THE ELVIS INTERVIEW
A SECOND CHANCE

AuthorHouse™
1663 Liberty Drive, Suite 200
Bloomington, IN 47403
www.authorhouse.com
Phone: 1-800-839-8640

AuthorHouse™ UK Ltd.
500 Avebury Boulevard
Central Milton Keynes, MK9 2BE
www.authorhouse.co.uk
Phone: 08001974150

©2006 M.J. Allan. All rights reserved.

No part of this book may be reproduced, stored in a retrieval system, or transmitted by any means without the written permission of the author.

First published by AuthorHouse 09/15/2006

ISBN: 1-4259-6204-1

Printed in the United States of America
Bloomington, Indiana

This book is printed on acid-free paper.

INTRODUCTION

ELVIS AARON PRESLEY took his last breath on August 16, 1977; sang his last song, played to his last audience and signed his last autograph. Millions of fans mourned him -- still mourn him years later. The giant of rock and roll music was no more. There would never be another king. There would never be another voice like his again. Today his home, Graceland, has been turned into a museum, a "shrine". His records are still selling, his movies still draw audiences and his popularity on television and video tapes continues to thrive. The American public remains loyal to their king. Stories are still being written about him and the networks still draw viewers when they run his television specials. In the minds of thousands he is still alive, still among us; some even say they have seen him while others claim to have spoken with him. Many fans continue to ask what really happened to him that night in August of 1977. One man who claims to have the answers to the query, "*whatever happened to Elvis Presley*," chronicles his fantastic encounter with a man called John. Bill Davis is a highly respected news reporter. Best known for his newspaper column and television shows, he has gained a reputation for integrity and honesty over the years. He was never known to be one-sided or predictable in his assignments. If this story is true, then he is responsible for holding the life of another human being in his hands or, perhaps, his future. Where did it all start? Are we soon to know what the truth is about Elvis Presley? Or are we just going to be reading fiction? You tell me!

A SECOND CHANCE

Chapter I

An early model Ford sedan winds its way along a narrow two-lane highway that runs parallel to the shoreline of a large fresh-water lake toward a small, sleepy retirement community. It is mid-October and rain splats against the windshield of the car in which the driver is the only occupant. Leaning forward, he stares into the wind-blown rain trying to pierce the black night as the windshield wipers slash at the rain, only momentarily clearing his view of the road. His eyes follow the wipers, thinking about their action -- first blurring the road and then clearing his view, constantly repeating this action -- almost mesmerizing him. It makes him think of his own mind; sometimes things are crystal clear and easily understood, then there are times when everything appears blurry. He struggles now to put into perspective what he is about to do. He has gone over the plan a thousand times, yet as the moment nears, it seems unreal, almost frightening. However, he has made his decision and he will follow through no matter what the consequences.

He arrives at his destination -- a small diner on the main street of town. Pulling up to the phone booth at the far end of the building, he stops, shuts off the engine, slowly opens the door, gets out and almost hesitantly approaches the booth.

Reaching into his pocket, he pulls out two items, one is a piece of paper with a phone number on it, the other is a small, round, black plastic device which he snaps onto the phone's mouthpiece. He dials the number and an operator from the NBC newsroom comes on the line.

"How may I direct your call?"

"Yes ma'am, I would like to speak with Bill Davis, please."

"May I ask who is calling and the reference to your business with Mr. Davis?"

"Just tell him I have information concerning the whereabouts of a well-known public figure who is supposed to have died many years ago ... but who is very much alive."

"Will you please hold, sir?"

"Yes ma'am."

As John waits for Davis, he pulls his jacket collar up closer to protect his face from the driving rain and cold wind."

"This is Bill Davis. What's this all about?"

"Well, sir, all I want now is ten minutes of your time. You may even want to hang up on me as I tell you about this, but please don't -- just hear me out. You are about to lock into the news story of this century."

"Go on, I'm listening."

"Several years ago I became friends with a man here in town, a man with an incredible past. He had once been the focus of millions of people all over the world. He would be instrumental in developing rock and roll music as we know it today. He was an incredible performer whose music appealed to almost everyone who heard him -- young, middle aged and old. His primary focus was on rock music, but for those with a more modest taste, he sang country music, and for the religious-minded, he put his talents into spirituals with the utmost sucess ... in everything he sang. Girls screamed and threw their bras, panties and room keys onto the stage. Men gritted their teeth in jealousy...."

Bill breaks into this historical dialogue and asks the caller, "Are you going somewhere with this?"

"I'm sorry sir; yes I am. Elvis Presley is still alive and lives right here just outside of town."

"Where is 'right here'?" Bill demands to know.

"I'll tell you that a little later."

"Okay, I'll wait, but for now, tell me why you're calling *me* about this?"

"Because he is very concerned about being exposed by some folks who live in this area. He feels that if it's to happen, he wants it presented the right way."

"And what is the right way?" Bill is quick to ask.

"I'm not exactly sure. He seems to think that if the story is to be told, he wants it written by someone like you. He feels confident you would tell it with dignity, honesty and compassion. If it could be done in this manner, then maybe there would be hope for his future -- to live the life he has now found."

"And what kind of life is that?" Bill presses for definitive details.

"Well, sir, a happy one. He is very content for the first time since he entered the entertainment business."

"Let me repeat what you're saying -- Elvis Presley is alive ... and well.... Okay, but before you tell me how and why, I'd like to tape the rest of this conversation ... then I'll probably hang up on you anyhow."

"No! No sir. I don't want you to record any of this, at least not right now."

"Okay, so I'll wait -- since I can't tape without your permission anyhow. What did you say your name is?"

"John, sir."

"John what?"

"Just John for now, sir."

"John, we seem to have a poor phone connection here. Your voice sounds raspy. Are you calling from a phone booth?"

"Yes I am, and it's pouring cats and dogs, so please -- just listen to me."

"Don't you have a phone at home? persists Bill.

"Yes, I do," comes the reply.

"Then why didn't you call me from that phone?"

John hesitates before answering. He thinks about his rise in anxiety during the past few months and about the possible exposure. Maybe he is over-reacting; possibly he is developing some sort of paranoia about all this. After all, he is calling from a phone booth and disguising his voice ... a necessary precaution due to the possibility that his own phone may be tapped.

Bill can't understand why he is still on the line with this nut, yet there is a feeling of something -- he can't quite pinpoint what it is, but his instincts are sharp. The reporter in him is always on the alert for a good story. It's not exactly in *what* this guy is trying to tell him, but in the way he's telling it. Bill interrupts the pause to ask why Elvis Presley isn't making this phone call himself, and asks if Elvis is aware that someone is about to break his story to a reporter? John doesn't know quite how to answer these questions. It was never his intention to make this phone call himself, much less speak in third person, but that's what he is doing and if he messes up his answers now, it can cause confusion, even cast doubt on the conversation -- Bill may not believe the truth and may even hang up on him.

John finally answers, "Well sir, I believe he will call you, but this first contact is very traumatic for him and in exposing himself too soon, he risks blowing the whole deal. After all, Mr. Davis, you need to understand that he is about to turn his life upside down once more -- life as he is living it now may not be possible once he opens the floodgates of publicity. How would you handle that? How would you feel?"

Bill's sarcasm, clearly evident up to this point, begins to soften. He is not sure why he is still on the phone, but he settles down to listen.

"Mr. Davis, is it so difficult to comprehend that under certain circumstances a man may wish to fake his own death in order to survive ... to live as he chooses? After all, sir, does not even the Good Book tell us that only in death can we really experience life?"

"Just where are you going with this, John?"

"My hope is that I can lead you into the truth about what *really* happened. I intend to tell you the facts that preceded and led to a master plan, or a hoax, as some will later refer to it. I will tell you what he hoped to gain and what resulted. If you are not able to justify its purpose after careful scrutiny of the facts and reasons for his actions, then all may be lost. I challenge you, sir, to reach deep into your soul and find the type of understanding we all need when we are in crisis and desperately searching for a solution. If the worst does occur, I may as well put a gun to my head and pull the trigger!

John's voice quivers with the emotion he feels. "The fact that a public figure, a super-star who has it all, would not want to live a normal life, like everyone else, would be far, far from the truth and I, or rather he, is living testimony to that premise. Vulnerability does not, by any means, touch only the weak or the poor. In fact, many successful folk are more apt to be vulnerable as they attain greater levels of success.

Bill starts to ask a question, but John stops him, saying, "I'm getting cold and the rain isn't letting up. I'll have to call you again later."

By now, not only Bill's interest but his curiosity has increased. He almost shouts into the phone, "When?"

"Tomorrow, about the same time."

"All right, I'll instruct my secretary to put you through."

"Thank you, sir. Good-bye for now."

John hangs up, removes the device from the receiver, jumps into his car and heads for home.

Bill sinks back into his chair and let's out a big sigh, murmuring, "Is there credibility here or am I the victim of a hoax? It's really not so idiotic; faking one's own death for various reasons is not a new concept. It's been tried before...and failed! But it's also been tried and succeeded! This could turn out to be an incredible story!" With these thoughts swirling around in his mind, Bill clears his desk and prepares to go home for the night.

Chapter 2

Soaking wet, John arrives home -- a modest ranch style house nestled back on three acres of wooded forest. It is in keeping with only two other homes in the immediate area. Inside, large wooden beams cross the ceiling, hardwood floors with throw rugs are neatly arranged for a warming effect and a large stone fireplace covers almost one entire wall. He spends a good deal of time just sitting and reading, or watching the flames crackle and change color. How simple his life had become -- finding pleasure in so simple a pastime.

John reaches the door, unlocks it and steps inside where he is immediately greeted by a large black and gray, furry Husky who stands up on his hind legs to kiss John's face, almost unbalancing him. The dog barks with happiness and John barks back. "Get down, Fur Face, I'm glad to see you too."

Sunny's tail wags from side to side and he rolls onto his back to have his tummy rubbed. John pets him and asks if he's hungry. He gets a loud bark in reply. The two head for the kitchen where Sunny's food is placed in his dish and quickly devoured. Meanwhile John pours himself a cup of coffee as he takes off his wet jacket. He walks through his living room to the double sliding glass doors which open onto a patio and garden and he looks out over the lake.

The rain has stopped and the moon reflects into a calm lake as it peeks through a break in the clouds. John sits down on a patio chair, sips his coffee, and begins to wonder about his conversation with the reporter. Sunny has finished his dinner and now prances out to sit beside John.

"Well, Sun, it's begun. Our lives may never be the same again after today. I have a good idea of what we may be in for. The question is, does Bill Davis believe my story? John takes a sip of his coffee before answering his own question. "Probably not right now, but he will." The dog stares at him, cocking his head from side to side as if trying to understand the words. "But how do you make the world understand? What do I say to Bill to get him inside my head? Will he be able to tell the story in such a way that people will realize and understand just what can happen to a person when he is under a great deal of pressure. The idea is not unique and the reasons may not be, but the results are vital for the preservation of life. How can that be wrong, Sun? If it is, then we are about to find out and possibly pay the supreme price. I guess ultimately happiness can have its price, eh, Sunny?"

John stands up, stretches, and heads for the bedroom. Sunny cocks his head waiting for John to say, "Let's go to bed, fellah," then follows him through the door leading to the bedroom. A photograph of Elvis with his mom and dad are on the night table. It is the only picture in the house which identifies with the past -- who he was before he arrived here. There is no other trace of memorabilia anywhere in the house to identify who he once was. For John, only the present and future are important; his previous life remains buried in a past which came to an end on August 16, 1977.

There *is*, however, another very visible item he has carried over into the present which could link him to his past life -- the old square box-style piano sitting against a wall in his living room.

As he gets ready for bed, he passes his mirrored dresser. He stops in front of it and stares at his reflection for a long moment. Running his hands through his medium length greying hair and stroking his well-groomed beard, he mutters, "I'm still not a bad-looking guy, huh, Sunny?" Twisting for a side-view of his body, he studies it for a minute, noting how slim he has remained, with just the slightest hint of a tummy, and mutters once more, "I didn't look like this when they said I had it all. Seems like having it all means different things to different people, right boy?"

John kicks off his bedroom slippers and drops back on his bed. In the flick of an eye, Sunny jumps up and sprawls beside him, just an arm's length below his master. He reaches down with one hand and pets his dog's head. His other arm rests across his forehead. With closed eyes, John's thoughts are now his own.

Life has become a puzzle again for John. The pieces, so carefully put back in place, were now beginning to fracture. Past, present and future are an unknown once more. John thought about how he must keep a good perspective on what the future may have in store as the result of his present decision. The details, however, have yet to become clear to him.

The horror of his almost forgotten past creeps into his conscious thoughts. Lights! Screams! Drugs! Money...! A fat man who sang his heart out and had the world by its tail! John did not want to remember the nightmare life he had left behind, but suddenly it is flooding his memory. Was the phone call responsible? Was he becoming paranoid with the possibility of exposure, or was he justifiably afraid that his neighbors, two people he scarcely knows, were about to shake up his future? Would they really do this to him, or was his phone call premature? He decides to call Mona in the morning and tell her about the call.

John's eyes are heavy with sleep now. He has mentally exhausted himself and drifts wearily into a restless sleep; tears stream from the corners of his eyes and slide down his cheeks ... John cries ... in the dark and alone and John ... Elvis Aaron Presley ... is finally asleep.

The next morning John wakes up early. A bright, crisp, late October morning is about to start the day. He showers and dresses, apparently in better spirits than he was the night before. As he pulls up his old, faded blue jeans, topped off with an oversized sweat shirt, he talks to Sunny, his 'sounding board'.

"Well, Sun, how do you feel about calling Mona? Maybe we could take a spin over there for breakfast ... what do you think? Sunny barks his approval, wagging his tail.

"All right then, we'll find out -- bring me the phone."

Sunny prances into the living room, picks up the receiver in his teeth and trots back to John.

"Good boy ... good boy."

John dials his friend's number and Mona answers.

"Hello?"

"Good morning, Mona. How would you like to have Sunny and me join you for breakfast?"

"Oh, I don't know ... does Sunny like pancakes and eggs?"

Laughing happily, John answers, "Sunny likes everything you make!"

"Well, then, come on over."

"Okay, we'll be there in about twenty minutes. See you then."

John hangs up, looks at Sunny and asks, "You do like pancakes and eggs, don't you? Sure you do -- it's Mona's cooking! Okay, let's go."

The road from his home to Mona's takes him along the coastline of the bay. Pine, oak and birch bark trees line the highway. As he drives through the small town, he is aware of how clean and well-kept it is, and thinks how happy he has been living here all these years. He turns to Sunny and says, "If I have my way, I'll die here. God has been good to me. Now, if he will only protect me for a few more years...."

"Oh well, whatever comes, we'll see it through together, won't we, old friend." Sunny barks in agreement as they turn into the drive and stop at the entrance. Mona opens the door, waves, and with a big smile, walks toward the car, greeting John with a big hug and a kiss on the cheek.

"Where have you been? I haven't seen you for awhile."

John replies, "Well, if yesterday constitutes a long time, then I've been busy ... and I'm fine!"

"Okay, okay. You know I always miss you."

Sunny barks, reminding her that he is there and wants to be greeted too.

"Okay, and you too, Sun," she laughs. "Well, let's go in, breakfast is waiting."

John puts his arm around Mona and the three of them walk toward the house.

The breakfast table is set up in the living room and there is a cheerful fire glowing in the fireplace.

John stops, stares into the flames and asks, "I know it's cool out, but a fire?"

Cheerfully, Mona answers, "Oh John, I just wanted to add some atmosphere to an ordinary breakfast."

"Actually, it's very nice," John tells her.

Mona serves the meal, then asks, "How did your day go yesterday?"

"Well, that's what I want to discuss with you."

"Oh? Is anything wrong?" Mona asks, looking worried.

"Maybe ... I don't know for sure, but I made that phone call."

Mona, now confused, asks which call?

"The one I've been thinking about for two years; the one you and I have been discussing from time to time."

Mona sits down and looks closely at John.

"I never did know whether or not you really would do it, but I'm not very surprised to learn that you finally did."

She hesitates, afraid to ask, but continues, "How did it go?"

"Oh," he sighs, "I wish I knew. I don't think he believes everything we talked about. I spoke as if I were a friend of Elvis', using the device I told you about to disguise my voice."

"Did you tell him ... everything?" Mona slowly asks, holding her breath.

"No, actually I said very little. I'm supposed to call him again this evening."

"John, you know there is no turning back if you do this?"

"I know ... I know...."

"Are you really so sure you might be found out?"

"We've talked about this before, Mona, and you know it's almost inevitable. If I can just get Bill Davis to do the story before anyone else, and do it with compassion and understanding, then maybe the public will also show some compassion, be understanding and forgiving."

"Do you really believe the public is capable of such generosity?"

John doesn't answer, instead he changes the subject.

"Listen, it's the weekend and it's a pretty day. Why don't we take your boat out and do a little fishing? Then we can have dinner out. We can talk more about this matter later."

He pauses, looks into Mona's eyes, then says, "I'm glad you are with me in this, Mona."

Chapter 3

John arrives home after spending the day with Mona. He putters around the house for awhile, then sits down to think -- yesterday's phone call was probably given very little thought by Mr. Davis. This time, though, he feels sure that if this second call is accepted, there will be many questions and he will have to reveal everything. However, he remains confident that what he is doing is necessary and right.

He reaches over and puts one hand on an old Bible which was given to him by his mother when he was a boy, telling himself, "My safety must lie here, no matter what they do." He picks up the phone receiver, only now he is not using the device. This time he will not be speaking in third person to Mr. Davis and there will be no turning back. John dials the number and the secretary answers.

"Hello, may I help you?"

"Yes ma'am. This is John. May I speak to Mr. Davis?"

"Oh yes, John. Mr. Davis is expecting your call; I'll put you right through."

John waits a few moments before Bill Davis answers.

"Hello, John. I wasn't sure you'd call back and in all honesty, I think I was hoping you wouldn't. I mean Elvis and all that!" Without a break in his voice, Bill asks, "Okay, mister, where do we go from here?"

John answers, "Well sir, there won't be any reason for you to doubt me after we finish this time; I can assure you of that."

Immediately the reporter notices the voice change and inquires about it. "There is something different in the sound of your voice, John. You sound remarkably like the fellow we have been discussing." With a smile on his face, he waits for John's reply.

"Yes sir, a few folks around here have accused me of that before. Some even go so far as to suggest I become an Elvis impersonator."

Quickly Bill responds, "Are you?"

"No sir, but you can be the judge of that as we proceed with this interview."

Bill asks, "Why is there a difference in the sound of your voice?"

"Well sir, I think maybe a little fear, a little paranoia, and a lot of unknowns, possibly phone taps ... I'm just a little scared about what I'm doing. I hope you can understand how difficult it is going to be for me -- I'm placing myself in a very vulnerable position."

"I suppose I can. Are you officially telling me now that you are Elvis Presley?"

John's answer is quick. "Not the one that the world is looking for. He is gone forever -- died in 1977. That, sir, is why it is so important for you to listen very carefully and to understand what I am about to tell you from here on."

"John, will you allow me to turn on my tape recorder for the rest of our conversations? I will need those tapes to do some checking and for verifying your story. You must realize the importance of having such a record to work from."

"I have nothing to hide now, sir. You may record anything you wish. However, you will not need to do research or look for verification; I'm all you need. From here on out it will be just you and me ... and one hell of a story!"

Bill asks John to wait a moment while he turns on the tape recorder.

"All right, John, I'm ready. You realize that I'm about to ask you a lot of questions? I expect you to answer them truthfully and comprehensively -- do you agree to that?"

"Yes sir."

"Good, okay John, let's start."

"You appeared, at the time of your supposed death, to be in no condition, at least mentally, to have arranged such a difficult (to say the least) deception. I mean, there had to be a lot of people involved; doctors, morticians and ambulance personnel, nurses, and so on. You were one of the most recognized men in the world. How could you have pulled that off?"

"I'm afraid, sir, that we are starting off in an area I will not tell you a lot about. I have given this a great deal of thought and am prepared to go to prison on this point. You can, I hope, appreciate the fact that if I were to disclose any names and the roles they may have played in this charade, they could be liable for their actions. I am not prepared to be responsible for sending anyone to prison for saving my life.

"I have been given a second chance by a small group of people who loved and cared enough about me to orchestrate a plan which could put them in jeopardy of going to jail if they were identified. I will, however, comment on some of the details of how, but with absolutely no comment on anyone who participated. That must be made absolutely clear and be acceptable to you before we can go on."

Bill again tells John how important it is to know what happened and who was involved.

"Everyone, your fans as well as the police, are going to demand this information. It's very important!"

John angrily replies, "No sir, it's not important! Why I did it is what's important! I have given a lot of myself to the public for many years. With all due respect to them and everyone who helped make me what I once was, I owe them nothing anymore. Everyone, and I do mean everyone, had to have a piece of me. Everyone had some of me but me, but that's all changed now!"

"Okay John. We'll drop it for now, but may come back to it later in the interview. May I ask if you thought up the idea yourself and directed it too?"

"No. Actually some close friends put the plan together. As you said earlier, I was not in a state of mind to even consider such a scheme, although

I was approached at some well-timed intervals for about a year and a half with various ideas of how we could successfully pull it off."

"What do you mean by "well-timed" intervals?"

"Well sir, they were more aware than I was that there were short periods of time when I was more receptive to listening and talking to them about the possibility of finding a way out of a life that was no longer working for me. In fact, it was killing me. You see, there were those who were aware of what was taking place in my life; some who knew I had a real heart and mind and that my own identity was being shattered.

"As far as those who knew me well were concerned, I was a robot without any sound reasoning of my own ... and they were right!"

Bill inquired about the eighteen months mentioned by John.

"Did you, at any point during that time, agree to their concept?"

"Obviously, yes. You see, while they were trying to persuade me to go along with their idea, they were already formulating the basis for my escape from this bondage ... eventually completing a fool-proof plan. The details took more than eighteen months to perfect and encompassed a solid back-up. If the original back-fired at some point, this back-up would be put into effect -- nothing had been left to chance ... this plan *was* my second chance."

Bill asked, "At what point did you agree to fake your own death?"

"Only in the brief moments when I was somewhat in touch with my own true feelings and reasonably sane -- which were rare. It was only at those times that I was in complete agreement with the idea. Again, sir, I might add that the timing was critical. They knew just when and how to approach me ... appealing to me during my brief periods of sanity. God bless them for that."

"What would have happened if you had not agreed?"

"There's absolutely no question about the outcome; I would really have been dead!" I understand that if I had backed out at the final moments of preparation, they might have kidnapped me in order to save me. And I will tell you this, sir, if the end result had to be what it appeared it would be, I would have had no problem with that plan, although it would have been considerably more difficult. Maybe it still wouldn't have worked if done that way, but I'm glad it didn't come to that -- having to be kidnapped, I mean."

"Why did it take a year and a half to plan?"

"Because there were a lot of things that had to be arranged in such a manner as to make it foolproof."

"Can you be more specific about the nature of the arrangements?"

John pauses before answering, then continues, "Well, there were bank accounts to be set up, a place to live and a location to dry out had to be found, and an in-depth screening process for persons who would have to be involved. Every aspect of this plan had to be perfect."

"Do you still maintain some kind of a relationship with any of those people?"

"I won't go into anything concerning prior personal relationships. I will tell you, though, that almost everything having to do with that time in my life was left behind."

Bill starts to ask another question when John politely interrupts, asking him to hold the line for a moment. "I just realized I forgot to feed Sunny."

"Sunny ... who is Sunny?"

"My dog."

"My God, John! You're telling me one of the news stories of the century and you want to interrupt that to feed your dog?"

"Yes sir."

"Okay John, I give up! I'll hold."

John puts the receiver down, walks to the kitchen, says a few words to Sunny as he grabs a can of dog food off the shelf in the cupboard. He opens it and empties the contents into Sunny's bowl.

While he waits, Bill sits back in his chair, puts his hand over the receiver and mutters to himself, "This guy has some sense of humor! He's in the process of turning his life inside-out and he wants to feed his dog."

He laughs and rearranges his notes. Jotting down some more questions, he says to himself, "I'm beginning to think this guy is for real!"

Chapter 4

John finally returns to the phone. "Mr. Davis, are you still there?"

"Yes, John, I'm still here. Why don't you just call me Bill from here on?"

"Sure Bill ... be glad to."

"So ... what type of dog do you have?"

"Oh, he's a big Husky. Been a good friend for a long time."

"Do you and Sunny live by yourselves?"

"Yes sir."

"Any girl friends?"

"I have a friend that I've been seeing for quite awhile now."

"Any plans for marriage?"

"Well, she would like that and I'm sure I would too. But with this hanging over me, I'm not sure this is the right time. If some things turn out well after this story hits the press, we'll probably get married. On the other hand, we may not have any future at all after this."

Bill changes the subject, sensing John's mood. "John, you mentioned a screening process. What actually did occur during the interactions with prospective participants?"

"It had to do with evaluating certain individuals to test their loyalty ...

you know, their ability to maintain confidentiality. They were fed small bits of information about the plan and then monitored for many months to see if they would leak that information out."

"I see. The planning, then, was quite thorough?"

"Oh yes. It was very carefully thought out."

Bill asks about the dry-out period and just what this involved.

"It was pretty traumatic. It consisted of a location where I would spend three months, or however long it took, to re-establish my own identity. I don't mean a name change or anything like that.

"It's difficult to explain. It was a debriefing or deprogramming process. It's where I was helped to get back in touch with reality. It enabled me to come back down to earth and see things from an ordinary, or a normal point of view and, well, to get rid of some very dangerous habits."

Bill asks, "Were professional people used for this?"

"Oh yes, I don't think this could have been handled by my friends alone. You have to understand this was pure hell for me and for those who were involved in counseling me through this ordeal. The process was very painful. I was sure at times that it would never end.

"As I said before, it was like a deprogramming. It seemed unreal, like a movie or a gruesome masquerade. I was screaming and fighting all the time. I wanted to go back. I didn't care that a crime had been committed.

"I didn't want to hear that I didn't exist in this world anymore. I missed my stardom. I was the king, not just the king of rock, but The King! I was untouchable -- I wanted for nothing -- and I believed that.

"Some of the time they would tell me that after the ordeal was over, I could go back if I wanted to. In fact, some of those involved really did want me to go back. Some thought that once I got a handle on things and started, or learned to exert a better sense of control, that I would definitely go back.

"Mr. Davis, I mean Bill, as we move along, I'll try really hard to describe what this whole thing was all about. I know my description and my words aren't coming out the way I would like them to, but please bear with me."

"Just take your time, John. I'm following you completely. I have no problem with your method here. I'd like to ask if you used a professional institution for your debriefing?"

"No, we didn't. We had given it some serious consideration, but decided there was too much risk involved. We found that it would be too difficult to approach an entire staff and trust them to maintain complete secrecy."

"So, where did you recruit your counselors and how were they chosen?"
"Well, sir, we just looked a little closer to home for that. We had come to know a great many professionals in all types of work over the years. We screened some of those people by feeding them information about a publicity stunt and how they could take part in it. The information was harmless, but they were to keep it a secret for an indefinite period of time -- until the stunt was ready to be used. They were then carefully observed to see if any of the information we

had given them was leaked out -- you know -- through press releases and other sources like that."

"A great deal of money must have changed hands for all this to be accomplished?" Bill's question went unanswered.

"That's not one of the areas I wish to discuss, Bill."

"All right, John. So where did the debriefing take place?"

"We had made prior arrangements to purchase a modest three bedroom house that was comfortable and well-suited to our needs."

"Where was it located?

John debates with himself for a moment whether he should answer this question, then realizes he and Bill will have to meet face-to-face to finish this interview. He knows the only way to dispel any shadow of doubt Bill may have about him must be settled when they meet. He also must be sure of Bill's intentions.

Maybe Bill won't tell the story as John wants it told -- with dignity, compassion, discretion and consideration. After all, he makes his living from headline stories -- stories which impact and use shock techniques, and not always with much thought for whom they may hurt in the process.

With this in mind, John finally answers Bill's question. "We bought a house just outside a semi-retirement town on the shore of Georgian Bay in Canada. I still live here today."

Bill is silent for a bit, then says, "I see -- so you picked Canada to start your new life?"

"Yes."

"John, during your treatment, were you allowed to go out or roam about as you pleased between counseling sessions? I can't help wondering what if you did have such freedom of movement, how could you prevent people from recognizing you?" Bill continues, speculating on the answer ... "a disguise of some sort, I suppose?"

"No, I was completely isolated. I was not allowed to leave for any reason. Being recognized was not the issue, however, they explained to me that it could be. Besides, if they had let me out of their sight, I might have tried to go back -- there's no doubt that I could. It might have gotten me some bad publicity, but then, publicity and such stunts are common in the entertainment business. I'm sure you're familiar with that kind of thing?"

"Yes, I am." Bill agrees.

"You know, John, you may wish to write a book, or have one written for you about this. It would be a fine way to back up this news story if timed to break with the media hype for its release. Then you'd be a man apt to educate the public to your way of thinking. How do you feel about that?"

"I'm way ahead of you. I've worked for about two years on it and completed it about two months ago. The fact is that it's based on an interview with a very well-known news reporter!"

Bill quickly asks, "How does it end?"

"You, sir, can tell me that. You'll know when this is over ... you'll know."

"John, let's go back to the isolation time frame again for a moment. Were you allowed any visitors? I mean, family, girl friends, any friends?"

"No. Just like everything else, it was a finely tuned part of the total plan. There were no contacts with anyone except the counselors, and one close friend with whom I was allowed to spend some time. He was the necessary link between me and them, the counselors, I mean. Even then, we were closely monitored by video cameras set up in the house and on the property. In fact, one of those cameras is still set up in my home as a reminder to me of one of the most traumatic three and a half months of my life. It was a time of great pain and of coming to terms with myself."

Bill leans back in his chair, gradually sinking down into it. His mind and muscles appear to be unloading an uneasy tension present since he first spoke to this man. Somehow, he feels a sense of relief -- finally sure of the unknown.

"You *are* Elvis Presley, aren't you?"

There is no tension in Bill's voice; just a seemingly ordinary question to which he finally believes he has the answer.

"Yes sir, I am ...", comes the reply, softly repeated, "... yes sir."

The phone is quiet now ... not a word can be heard, not even a sigh. Both men know exactly what is taking place over a telephone separating them by three thousand miles as each feels the heavy responsibility they now share.

Things will be different now. There's a certain bond, a trust has been established between them; a reliance upon each other. Neither knows just what the outcome will be, but each knows exactly what will be needed from the other to continue their relationship.

Somehow, now it is no longer John, or Elvis Presley and a reporter; it's one man's life placed in the safekeeping of another man's hands. John has to be himself; it's what he wishes to remain. Bill needs to fully understand the complete story and hold it up either for interpretation or for ridicule. Can he find a way to keep the world off John's back? It has certainly become a very delicate and complicated situation.

Bill finally breaks the silence. "John, we have to meet. I can be there in two days. How do you feel about that?"

"I guess it's time, huh?"

"Great! I need to tie up some business ends, but can leave here on Friday, if that's convenient for you. I'll need an address.

John feels a momentary doubt, then gives Bill his address. "Bill, you will come alone, won't you?"

"Absolutely. Do you mind if I bring a video camera?"

John's answer breaks the tension in this long phone conversation. "Oh no, there are lots of things to photograph out here."

"Funny, John, very funny. The only thing I want on this camera is you and this story."

The mood has changed, the strain of doubt has been laid to rest, and John quickly answers, "Right on! I'll see you on Friday, and Bill ... thanks. Good bye for now."

Chapter 5

Bill unplugs his tape recorder, grabs his coat and leaves his office. He walks quickly through the news room with its clattering typewriters and ringing telephones. Reporters are sitting at their desks doing follow-ups and gathering last minute information to finish their stories. Little do any of them know, as Bill walks by, that he carries the beginning of the 'story of stories'.

He is carrying the tape recording of a partial interview with a ghost, a man who doesn't exist anymore, a man whose music is still played all over the world, a man who had a tremendous impact on the music industry.

This man's music touched just about everyone who heard it in one way or another. Those who didn't care for rock music were suddenly jolted when he would sing a country song. For those who didn't care for either, he would hit the record shops with spirituals, selling everything he produced.

There was no single-mindedness in his music. He successfully appealed to all who heard him sing, who denied his death, saying they still heard him, listened to him, and enjoyed the music of the man they called "the King."

Even the young people of today's top music sounds are more than familiar with his unique style, the stage presence of his swivel hips, and his lip that curled-up as he sang or spoke. The Elvis drawl, the fanfare and the showmanship still make the females swoon in whatever medium he appears ... and, oh, those terrible movies! Bill thinks to himself, "I'll have to ask him about those."

Bill's thoughts are interrupted by the voice of his friend and executive producer. "Bill, can I see you a minute before you leave?"

"Sure, Ken, just give me a couple of minutes and I'll be right there."

Bill remembers he has forgotten something. He walks back toward his office, stops at his secretary's desk and asks her to make a reservation for him on a flight to Toronto, Canada.

"Oh, and a video camera too, please."

"Sure, when do you want to leave and return?"

"That's a good question, Ann. I'm not sure of the return date, so just leave that open if you can. I'll be leaving on Friday, a morning or early afternoon flight will do just fine, but morning would be preferable. Thanks, Ann, and don't forget the camera."

"I'll get right on it," she replies. "May I ask if this is a business or pleasure trip?"

"Let's just say it will be a pleasure to do business with this fellow."

"All right, Bill. I should have your tickets for you in the morning."

"Thanks again. Have a good night and I'll see you tomorrow."

Bill turns in the direction of Ken's office. They have been friends for a long time and worked together off and on for many years.

Bill had mentioned the phone call he'd received earlier in the day to Ken and got the same reaction he himself had felt after John's first call. It was not an unexpected response, although Bill did not let on that he, too, had put a small amount of stroke in the call. After all, reporters deal in facts and both of them were well aware of the media hype about Elvis. They knew about the numerous television programs and specials, about anonymous phone calls from 'Elvis', and from others who reported seeing him here and there. I'll bet Ken thinks maybe this call [John's] was tried before and it wasn't followed up. He tugs on his chin, thinking about that possibility as he slowly walks toward Ken's office ... I wonder....

Bill knocks on the door once.

"Come on in, Bill." Entering Ken's office, he is greeted with a question, "Where have you been the last couple of hours?"

"Oh, on the phone."

"Not with that spook you told me about?"

"Yep, but I don't think that spook is a spook!"

"Tell me you're not serious!"

"Ken, I want to go up there and interview him."

Ken sounds agitated as he responds, "Interview who? Go up where? Bill, you're crazy. You're acting like one of those rookies outside my door. This is not like you."

"I hear what you're saying, Ken, but there is something to this guy.

I don't know what it is, but I have to find out."

"What you're going to find out is that some nut thinks he's Presley! Hell, man, he probably called you from some mental institution; maybe he's laughing at you right now. That is, if he's even aware of having made the call at all."

"That's a possibility ... but I'm going anyway."

"Bill, sit down a minute -- let's talk straight. What is there about this guy that makes you consider for even a moment that he's telling the truth? I mean, how did he get to you in the first place?"

"Ken, listen to me. It isn't exactly what he said, it's how he said it. Not only how he said it, but the way he spoke. It was as if he was in some sort of pain. You know, there was some depth to his voice ... some heart to what he was telling me. There is some credibility to this and I'm going to do a follow-up!"

"Credibility! How much credibility does a dead man have? You are just as aware as I am of the media hype since his death -- the reported sightings, the telephone calls -- just like the one you got. Did he also have the voice to go along with the story? I'm right, aren't I?"

Before Bill can answer, Ken continues, "Hell, man, we even thought of doing a show on that one. Do you remember -- it was about a year ago? We discussed the prospect of doing the show for about five minutes and then spent ten minutes laughing about it -- don't you remember that?

"Yes I do, and the only reason we were going to put it on was because some of the networks were already doing it and getting good audience ratings. But what did we decide, you were there ... that we didn't want to be tied to the kind of audience that thrived on flamboyance. We didn't need to do this sort of fantasy story to hold on to our reader and viewer audience."

"If you're finished, then let me tell you that I'm going to do a follow-up. I've been wrong before and may be again, but I'm going. If it's all smoke, then I'll lose a couple of days, that's all!"

"All right ... all right, Bill, let's give him the benefit of the doubt for just a minute. How did he pull it off, and why did he do it?" How did one of the most recognized men in the world keep himself from being caught all these years, and what possible motive did he have for such an incredible hoax?

"I, for one, can only think of one -- publicity -- and that theory goes right down the drain because of the risk of severe litigation if he turned up and admitted to a publicity stunt like that. I mean he, and whoever else may have been involved, would still be in jail. So why would he do it, did he tell you that?"

"No, not yet, but he's going to. In fact, he told me that the method of how he pulled it off wasn't the important aspect. He said the *reason* for doing it was the issue here, and that's what he wanted me to focus in on. He is also aware of the consequences of what might happen if he is found out."

"This is idiotic!" Ken is still hot about the issue. He notices the recorder Bill is holding and asks if he had taped the conversation.

Bill was about to answer 'yes', but he stopped, hesitated and said "'No', it's just some material on another story."

"All right. Let's just say for the sake of argument that this guy is legitimate, which he is not, but let's say he is. I want you to send me the first bit of information you get. I mean, I want you to *express* me the first video of your interview. Understood?" Ken is still very upset about Bill's wild goose chase and goes on, his anger mounting along with his voice.

"I'll have his face and story all over the television networks, newspapers and magazine covers! I'll hang this guy out to dry! Elvis Presley or not, I'm sick and tired of these nuts and impostors. If they want a story, I'll give them more than they bargained for, and if this fellow turns out to be Presley, I'll see to it that he gets just what's coming to him. If anyone wants to have an interview after I'm finished with him, they'll have to do it in his jail cell.

"So if there's anything to this, I want to hear about it right away! Is that perfectly clear, Bill?"

"Yes, perfectly." It also became clear to Bill just why John wants the story to be done his way. John is the result of what publicity can accomplish, he understands the importance of a well released series of facts and information; how to prevent, or avoid the kind of press Ken has in mind.

Bill looks at Ken and says, "This is my story and I intend to do it my way. If you choose not to work with me on it, then I'm sorry, but I'm will still do it my way."

Bill's attitude has turned to disappointment and anger. He has worked with Ken for a long time and cannot believe he was viewing this issue with so much negativism. If the interview confirmed John's story, then Ken was about to feed him to the lions. How was he going to prevent this from happening? If John's story was credible, then he deserved to be heard and to have his story presented to the world in a just manner.

Bill's thoughts are interrupted by more of Ken's probing questions. "Where does this Elvis live? Where does he hang up his guitar these days?" Ken's sarcasm is becoming a little too much for Bill now. He wants no more of it!

Bill gets up from his chair and starts for the door, but Ken's voice follows him, "Where did he call you from?" Ken keeps pushing, "Somewhere in Canada outside of Toronto? Where outside Toronto?"

Bill knows at this point that there's no way he will release anymore facts relating to the story. He quickly thinks up a story and replies, "I'm not sure. He told me I'd be contacted at the airport on my arrival and given further directions. He also wants to be sure I'm alone."

"Fine, Bill. You go, but be back here in no more than five days. We have a show to do -- and keep me posted! I want to know exactly where you are and what's going on when you get there. Do I make myself clear?"

"Yes, perfectly clear." Bill resents Ken's tone of voice as well as his hostility. This entire meeting has upset him and he's glad to leave Ken's office.

Chapter 6

Bill arrives at the office the next morning to pick up his plane tickets and camera. He tells Ann, his secretary, that he won't be in the rest of the day in order to prepare for his business trip which includes gathering up background information on his story.

"Will I be able to reach you on your pager, Bill?

"No, not unless it's an emergency, otherwise, I don't want to be disturbed."

"But what if Ken ..., Ann gets no further before Bill interrupts, "Not even Ken. Is that clear?"

"I understand. I'll do my best to keep you from being paged for business."

"Thank you, Ann, I know you will use good judgment."

Bill leaves the office and spends the rest of the day visiting the local book shops. He picks up some material on Presley's life, then phones some of his contacts and fellow reporters on the subject of the supposed sightings and apparent phone calls made by Presley himself. He also reflects on his conversation with John. Funny, Bill is sure he heard John speaking in third person, yet he seemed to be talking about himself.

His voice sounded very raspy, with a distinct though faint southern drawl in it. He was also extremely polite and seemed to be in complete control of what he was trying to say. And then there was the emotion -- very apparent. You can't hide anxiety and emotion like he heard. Bill was experienced enough to judge effectively when someone was trying to bluff. Or was he?

After several phone calls, Bill could find no credibility to the supposed calls or sightings. He learned that the rumors were just that; not even a hint of anyone believing these false accounts was on file. He heads home to continue his reading, stopping at a fast food restaurant. At home, he settles down to read the material he has gathered on the man known as "the King".

Time passes quickly and before he realizes it, most of the night is gone. It is 3:30 in the morning and he has been reading for over nine hours. "I'd better get some sleep; I've got a plane to catch tomorrow," he mumbles. Then a light goes on in his brain as he realizes that tomorrow is today! Preparing for what is left of the night, he retires.

Waking up around nine o'clock, Bill quickly showers, dressing as he packs his overnight bag and calls a cab. Before walking out of the apartment, he calls his office to check for messages. Arriving at the airport with a little time to spare, he checks in, then stops for a cup of coffee while waiting impatiently for the plane. Before long his flight to Toronto is announced and he is first in line to board it.

Once on board, and having located his first class seat, he settles down for the long flight. After a short delay, the aircraft taxies to its assigned runway for takeoff. The plane vibrates as the throttles are pushed forward and then picks up speed for lift-off. He always enjoys flying; the power of a machine to lift off the ground and deliver its passengers to their destination safely and comfortably never ceases to amaze him.

As the aircraft reaches its cruising altitude and the seat belt sign goes off, Bill sets his seat into full recline position and thinks about how this flight is somehow different from his other business trips. This time it was not just taking him to a destination, but to where he would come face-to-face with a man presumed to be dead! Seeing Elvis Presley alive would prove beyond the shadow of a doubt his incredible claim; it may even be carrying him back in time.

Bill closes his eyes and his thoughts drift back to what has transpired. Instinctively, he feels that what he is doing is justified. However, he knows there are pieces of the puzzle which still need to be put in place. The story is unconfirmed and incomplete, yet his mind dares to relax and fantasize ... what does he look like after all these years? Bill laughs out loud; probably fat with two puffed out cheeks and long grey sideburns -- down to his ankles.

Bill is not amused for long, not even by his own humor. What does he really look like? What does he do? How does he live? Who knows his identity, and most of all, why? ... Why did he do it? The whole world was at his feet. He had millions of fans and many friends. Why would he want to fake his own death? Why not just retire? Bill asks himself and then attempts to answer his own questions, but the answers evade him -- they are all merely speculation. "Why don't I relax and just wait for him to give me the answers."

However, the wheels keep turning and his thoughts drift from his own questions to when he first heard of Elvis Presley. He was about thirteen then and can remember sitting in front of a black and white television screen. "I think it was on the Tommy Dorsey Show." His facts might be clouded, but it doesn't matter, he is just reminiscing.

"In my first introduction to rock and roll music, I sat there on the floor with my legs crossed and was utterly fascinated by this wild singer. I remember that everything in my life connected with this one appearance. I was to follow his music and the music of other rock and roll stars for many, many years after that first time. The next thing I knew, I was trying to gather up enough money to hitch-hike twelve miles to a theater just to see him on-screen in *Love Me Tender*.

"In those days my family didn't have very much money. We came from a very small resort town where everything of importance was a long way off; movies, theaters, restaurants, clothing stores and the usual sights and sounds teenagers longed to see and have. For spending money, my brother and I would search beneath the steps of the local vacation cabins that were only occupied seasonally. We'd find the change that had dropped between the slats of the front and back wooden entrance steps. Our many hours at this pastime were rewarded with enough coins to take us to the movies and buy some treats.

"Now that I think about those times, I'm not sure whether I liked *Love Me Tender*. I seem to recall wanting Elvis to sing more. What I do remember vividly are the ten Fudgicles I had at ten cents a pop while I watched the screen."

Bill also wonders how many thousands of grownups, in their childhood, were as influenced by Elvis as he was. "We danced with our girl friends in the school gym, softened by colored ceiling lights which revolved. We used to sit on the porch steps on warm summer evenings, either alone or with friends, listening and dreaming. Elvis made us think of faraway places and lands we had read about and only dreamed of ever seeing. He took us into a fantasyland of music and good times. We wondered what it would be like to be like him, to go where he went and do what he did, to sing like only he could sing."

It was a time of innocence; a time of dreams and hopes that would impact the rest of our lives in one way or another. Bill smiles as he remembers and says to himself, "I think the world would like to see him alive. Maybe that's why so many can't accept his death. He represents that time in our lives when we were young and had stars in our eyes; seeing, hearing and learning new things.

"For those of us who grew up with the sounds of early rock and roll, it was the best of times. Could it be that with his passing, those early years were also buried? For some of us, maybe this is unacceptable. Why should this giant of entertainment be allowed to die and take with him the memories and hopes of happy days that were once a part of our lives? How dare he take that away from us?"

A new thought interjects itself into Bill's thoughts. He sits up straight! Could this be the basis for Ken's negative reaction? Perhaps Ken's anger wasn't just about a wild goose chase; maybe he was unknowingly, or subconsciously representing those people who really may have resented his death? After all, Elvis did mean different things to different people.

As a news reporter, my job was to look at the various angles of a story and seek out the truth.

"You know," Bill tells himself, "even though the reported sightings of him and the silly phone calls he was presumed to have made were fairly obvious pranks, they too could have been just another way of saying we won't let him die. He touched so many people, we just can't let that happen."

With that thought, Bill decides he needs a little sleep. It was a long night and a long and interesting day still lay ahead of him, full of unknowns and questions to be answered.

John was not so fortunate. Sleep had not come easily for him that night. He had tossed and turned, experiencing nightmares and dreams that had not plagued him in years. Although John did have periodic flashbacks, not all of them were bad. He had maintained well over the last decade and a half and seemed to have succeeded in controlling his thoughts of good and bad times long ago. But last night was a reflection of the bad times. He had gone through this often for many months after his debriefing (as he referred to the ordeal).

On this bright, crisp Friday morning he awoke completely soaked in sweat. As he threw aside the bedclothes and swung his legs onto the floor, he placed his elbows on his knees and started to drop his sweat-soaked face into his hands when he noticed Sunny sitting up straight as a statue. His black and grey furry face with its piercing black eyes were staring into John's face. He thought, if a dog could have such a thing as concern written plainly on its face, then Sunny surely had it. John had an urge to laugh as he patted Sunny's head, but he controlled it. Instead, he just greeted his dog with a good morning and told him how thankful he was to have such a quiet, non-judgmental friend.

"You're always there, aren't you, Sun. No matter where I go or what I do, you are always there to be my friend. I just wish you could help me with what lies ahead. If only I could be sure that I'm not taking this a step too far. If only I could know that what I'm doing is the right thing ... and how it will work out. Well, whatever happens, Sun, we're going to do this alone."

John speaks with self-assurance, repeating, "We're going to do this alone. I won't let my past connections help, I want no part of that." John is referring to those friends who helped get him out of the business nightmare. He means no disrespect to any of them, he is simply determined to handle whatever comes up in John's life by himself, without striking up old ties.

Chapter 7

John is not expecting Bill until late afternoon and decides he and Sunny might as well spend the day fishing, one of their favorite pastimes. John has always loved the water and since living here by a large blue and green colored fresh water lake, he has enjoyed a great deal of his time both on the lake as well as in it. He didn't have many opportunities to enjoy the simple things in life prior to arriving here; after all, he had lived in a fantasy world where nothing was real.

He remembers learning to ski for one of his films, and he still enjoys the sport. He also knew very little about fishing, but has now developed quite an appetite for it. John has developed many new interests which provide him with everything it takes to be happy.

As John drives through the town on his way to Mona's house, he is very aware of the autumn colored blanket of reds, yellows and golds covering the trees, and thinks out loud, "There's so much beauty to enjoy in the world; all one has to do is take the time to see it."

He wonders why people strive so hard to find the American Dream when it's already in full view. Why does everyone want to reach the top of the mountain when there is so much beauty in the valley at eye level, just waiting to be discovered anew each season and steeped in its own beauty. If we would just look around we'd see it, enjoy the touch it and smell it, he thinks to himself.

Each day God renews our life, yet we live in blindness, discontent and unhappy, not seeing the treasures all around us. How can we expect to attain true happiness unless we stop along life's path to reap the beauty of his other miracles, like inhaling (he breathes deeply) the freshness of each new day, the beauty of a flower, a sunrise or a bird's song? How often do we bother to watch a breathtaking sunset? ... all are God's miracles ... we're just so busy dashing around ... that we neither see nor treasure the beauty surrounding us.

If asked, I would be the first to admit my own lack of insight. Not only was I blind, but I didn't hear a bird sing or feel the velvety softness of a flower between my fingers. I was narrow of mind, without appreciation for the gifts bestowed upon me -- I was without sight, but now I see. Never again will I want or desire all those things I once had. For me having has become not having.

They arrived at the dock where John, Sunny and Mona greeted each other with an affectionate hello and a hug. "What are you fellows up to today?" Mona wants to know.

"Well, I thought that since you're working, me and old Fur Face here would take your boat out and bring us back a fish dinner for tonight, do you mind?"

With a grin, Mona says, "No, not at all. She's all gassed up and rarin' to get started. Why don't you come on in for a few minutes first?"

"Sure." As they enter, John says, "What's up?"

"Well ... why don't you tell me?" she asks anxiously.

"Tell you what?" John replies, knowing full well what Mona's question is all about.

"You know what I mean! ... Is he still coming? ... What happened?"

"Yes, he's coming. He'll be here this afternoon about six. I think he's flying into Toronto and renting a car ... might pick up a motel, too, but I may ask him to stay with me if he wants to. It may help him get a better feel for me and some of the things I would like for him to see ... about the way I live now. I'm hoping I won't have to explain every detail; that he'll pick up on some of the subtleties of what and how I'd like him to do this story. You understand, don't you?"

"Yes, I think so. You don't want to just be interviewed and answer a lot of questions; you'd like him to experience the way you live as well. Yes, I think that might be the best approach. John, *you know, don't you*, that I'll be there and do anything I can to help you. Do you want me to be there tonight?"

John walks over to Mona and gently grasps her hands. Squeezing them as he smiles at her, he says, "I know you'll be there. You're always there for me and I love you for it, but I think I'd like to meet him alone. I'm not sure how things will go tonight. In fact, I'm very nervous about this meeting."

"Isn't that strange, John? You've faced thousands of people, singing and performing for them, you've met with all kinds of people, politicians, actors, a variety of businessmen -- yet you feel nervous about talking to one reporter?"

With a 'theatrical' stern look, John replies, "Those were different times!" Then, looking remorseful, he says, "I'm sorry, honey, I shouldn't be flippant about this; it is very serious ... just couldn't resist the temptation."

"I know, and I'm glad you still have a sense of humor. Don't worry about it. Let's go in, I'll get us some coffee."

They walk through her office, where she conducts her rental business, and enter her living quarters. She purchased her home about five years before she met John. Her property boasts a beautiful house facing the lake and as it includes its own boat dock, Mona decided it might be interesting to turn one of the front rooms into a rental office for water skiers and visiting fishermen. The demand was there and she would enjoy the activity. She hadn't intended for it to be a thriving business, just something to keep her occupied. She managed to keep her own hours and maintain her privacy. John and Mona found time to spend many summer days on the water together. Neither of them ever seemed to tire of the pleasure the lake gave them.

They sat at the kitchen table now, sipping freshly brewed coffee. Sunny lay on the floor near John's feet.

Mona looked out through the bay window across the shimmering lake.

"It's so beautiful and peaceful, isn't it?" she remarked.

John didn't answer immediately. He just stared at her and thought, "She's what is beautiful." Her dark, medium length hair had only a hint of gray in it; she was considerably younger than he and this bothered him at first, but disappeared as their relationship solidified. She was a joy to look at and fun to be with.

Finally he stands up, walks over and leans down to plant a kiss on her cheek. Lovingly, he says, "You are a very special lady!"

"Thank you, John, you make it very easy for me to feel special." Mona replies with a warm smile and shining eyes.

"Mona, you know those bad dreams I told you about? ... yes, well -- I had another one last night. I think they may be coming back. I woke up this morning in a cold sweat. I thought I had done with that long ago; now I wonder if this is the beginning of what's ahead ... all over again. With the exception of one family in this town, this nightmare might have remained buried forever. I just don't know anything for sure anymore. After tonight, I can only speculate about the future. I was determined to maintain control over this from the first time I ever considered calling Bill. Now, I just don't know."

"Honey, you know it's not unusual for one to have flashbacks under such circumstances." Mona stops ... then continues,

"You ... *we*, have some unknowns to deal with that wouldn't be easy for anyone, let alone you, who have had an extremely different kind of life than most of us. What you experienced was unique; only time will heal all the wounds and the anxiety you have endured ... it's not easy to escape totally from the fears and distress you are experiencing, but when it's all over, you will find peace again and be able to move forward with your life ... as *you* want to live it.

"You have become an extremely strong man as a result of those years, so why not take it one day at a time. Isn't that what you've been doing for a lot of years now? Why let something which may never even occur ruin the life you have so carefully rebuilt? Remember, no one really knows what tomorrow has in store, so why not let tomorrow take care of itself. Okay?" Mona's voice is gentle and reassuring.

John knew she was right. He hugs her tightly and whispers, "Thanks." Then, in a more cheerful tone, he says, "Lemme have the keys to the boat, hon, and we'll be off."

Mona gently pushes John away and laughs, "I just love that Elvis accent and the way you say 'lemme'. Say it again."

John is amused by her sense of humor. "She always seems to lighten up a harsh moment. What do you think, Sun? No fresh fish for Mona!" Sunny wags his tail furiously and barks once.

"C'mon, Sun, let's go catch us some fish."

Mona walks out to the boat with them. "You know, John, the summer is over. I think I'll dry-dock the boats next week -- I'm only getting a few rentals now and then from some fishermen. Can you give me a hand with closing down?"

"You bet! Just let me know which day you want to get started."

They arrive at the dock and John unties the boat. "Get in, Fish Face." Sunny's tail wags joyously as he jumps into the boat.

Mona laughs, "Who do you keep calling him "Fish Face?"

John ignores her question, as if refusing to hear it. Instead, he looks at her and smiles, "You'd be the prettiest fish I ever saw. I'll see you in a while."

"Okay, have a good time. I've got to bring the books up to date or I'd go with you," Mona responds to his quip.

"That's okay, I'm just looking for a little open space for awhile," John calls back as he starts the motor, waves to Mona and shoves off.

Mona shouts as he pulls away, almost as an afterthought and betraying her true thoughts, "God has been good to us. Why would he stop now?"

Her voice is drowned out by the noise of the throttle John has pushed forward. Sunny is perched with his hind legs on the seat, his front paws on the bow and his tail upright. He is looking straight into the wind as it blows his ears back parallel to his spine. John yells to Sunny, "You look like you are about to lead a cavalry charge!"

Sunny turns his head as he looks back at John, then straight out again.

The weather is good, but carries a strong hint of the winter ahead. They soon arrive at one of John's favorite fishing spots near a small island. It is one of many dotting this part of the lake. He shuts down the engine and prepares a rod for casting.

"Some good fishing here!", he tells Sunny. Sure enough, after a very short time, John hooks a good size fish and reels him carefully in toward the boat.

"Got a good one, Sun," he reports to Sunny. Then, as the fish is brought to within four or five feet of the boat, he sees the flash of his dog leaping over the side. SPLASH! Sunny had decided to do the retrieving personally.

"Get out of there, I'll lose him! Get out of there!" John screams frantically. But Sunny ignores him and continues to splash and bite at the fish dangling on the hook. John can't reel him in, but Sunny is finally able to grab the slipping catch. With the fish in his jaws, he swims toward the boat just as proud as a new father who has just been told it's a boy; holding the fish up for John's approval.

"We are not shooting ducks, Fur Face," John scolds. "This is called fishing and it's not a team effort." Stretching, he pulls Sunny back into the boat, not a little annoyed that he is now soaking wet.

After three or four hours of this 'catch-and-splash' fishing game, they call it a day and head back to the pier.

None of the fish they've caught are kept -- all get a reprieve when they were thrown back into the lake still alive. John just wanted to fill a few hours with something that would take his mind off the upcoming meeting with Bill Davis. They reach the dock and John ties off the boat, grabs his fishing gear and walks to the house. As he opens the door, he sounds off, "Anyone home?"

"I'm in here," Mona shouts back, "how was your fishing expedition?"

John replies, "Great ... just fine!"

Mona notices that John's jacket and pants are wet. "What happened, did you fall into the lake?", she laughingly asks.

"No, but I might as well have. Sunny decided he wanted to help bring in the catch for me and I spent most of my time pulling him back into the boat."

Mona and John sit and talk for awhile, then John and Sunny leave. He tells her he'll call her later or tomorrow.

"Okay, honey, good luck."

John hugs Mona tightly, saying, "Thanks, I'll need all the luck you can spare."

By the time they arrive back at the house, the weather has turned cold and there, sitting on the front steps waiting for John, is Bill Davis. John sees him and immediately there's a lump in his throat. He begins to speak as he walks toward Bill, "Bill Davis?"

"In the flesh, cold flesh, that is. Elvis Presley, I presume?"

"John Baker will do just fine," is his reply.

Chapter 8

Bill grasps John's hand tightly, shaking it as he looks into John's face. He stares at him for a moment as if trying to look through the salt and pepper beard and mustache, "You really are...."

"Yes, I am," interrupts John.

Bill is thrilled ... not his usual character ... and almost child-like in his delight as they reach the house.

"I'll be! ... you really are!" Bill can't help repeating as if he is seeing a ghost. "You did it...! You're really alive!"

"Yes sir. Oh, by the way, this is Sunny."

"Ah, this is the dog you had to feed right in the middle of our long distance telephone conversation."

John laughs, "Yep, that's him. Why don't you hang your coat on that rack by the door and come on in."

"Thank you. You know, John, I can see why you don't have a problem with being recognized -- your greying hair ... the beard, and all.... You've managed to keep yourself in pretty good shape ... certainly don't look anything like you did the last time I saw you."

"Well, sir, I would hope not," he smiles, "that was fifteen years ago."

John changes the subject, "How was your trip?"

"Just fine, but I really enjoyed the drive out from the airport -- the countryside up here is really beautiful. I can see why you chose this location as your home for the future."

"Make yourself comfortable while I start the fire. It's a little chilly tonight; guess the first signs of winter have chosen this weekend to arrive -- along with your arrival."

While John is busy at the fireplace, Bill questions him about the local motel facilities. John explains about the motel just on the edge of town. "It's not fancy, but clean and the folks running it are very nice. But why don't you stay here? I have lots of room and you are more than welcome. Besides it might work out better for our purpose. I'd like you to get a good feel for the way I live now", he hesitates, then continues, "... the way I'd like to continue living."

"Thank you for the invitation, John, I'd like very much to stay here with you."

"Good, then it's settled. When's the last time you ate?" John asks as he lights the fire.

"As a matter of fact I haven't had anything to eat since breakfast, except for a snack on the plane, which wasn't much."

"Well then, how about we get the grill going? I cook a mean hamburger."

Bill agrees, saying, "Sure ... it sounds great to me."

"Okay, you just relax. I'll hit the patio and you just get acquainted with this ole' house. Bedroom's the second door on the left. You probably would like to wash up after your long ride."

"Yes, I would. Oh, by the way, John, I've decided not to tape the interview for now. We can pick up on that later."

"Sure it's okay, though I don't quite understand why not. However, you're the reporter, so whatever you think is best is best with me too."

"I'm not exactly sure myself, John, but we can just do a relaxed face-to-face for now and get to know one another first."

John continues the preparations and when Bill returns they continue their conversation.

Bill, now that he is more relaxed, starts to take notice of the surroundings. "I see you have a piano. Do you still sing?"

"Yes sir. Call me John, please. Yeah, I still sing, but now the choice is mine. I mean ... I sing what I like, when I like, and mostly for me, not for an audience of one hundred thousand or more screaming fans."

"I see," answers Bill, adding "You didn't enjoy performing?"

"Oh, I loved it! Don't get me wrong. Before I go on with this, I'd like to emphasize that from here on in, I'm going to be trying to tell you ... and the world, I guess, just why I did it. It's probably going to be the hardest part of the interview. I mean ... sometimes the simplest things are the most difficult to explain or to understand.... Those burgers will be done any time now."

"John, let's go back to where the problems started. I mean, when did you feel there was something wrong with the life you were living?"

"That's a relatively easy one to answer. It went all the way back to when I became aware that I was in the big time. I remember an interview with a reporter, or was it a disk jockey -- I'm not sure which, but he asked me where I was going from 'here'-- like, what were my future plans? I remember hesitating before I answered his question. Bill, I didn't hesitate about the business aspect of his question; it was something deeper inside of me that I felt.

"Even though I was at the beginning of my career, at that moment I sensed there was something ahead if me that wasn't quite right. My answer to him was that I wasn't quite sure.

"Everything was moving so fast from that time to when I left the business that I never had the time to look at the future ... to find out what I really wanted for myself. Oh, there were brief moments -- when my mom was alive -- but those were the only times I was able to think clearly about the business, my family, and just where the great American dream was taking me."

John serves the food and continues his thought. "I'll tell you this though, I don't believe for an instant that the American dream is all it's cracked up to be. *This,* where I am now, is my American dream." He spreads his hands out, directing Bill's attention to the surroundings. "This house, this country, my dog, my friend, even this fire that you see here, Bill ... something as simple as a crackling fire means more to me now than just keeping warm. It's a recreational pastime, my relaxation and I spend hours just enjoying it all. Sounds funny, doesn't it?"

"No, John, I don't think it's funny at all. What you said about the American Dream ... I guess it just means different things to different people."

"Maybe so, but I know -- or thought I knew -- what it was. I chased it, caught it, and almost let it destroy me.... How's the burger?"

"Very good, thanks. Do you do most of your own cooking?"

"Yes, I do. It's something I had to get used to and over the years I've learned to enjoy doing it."

"John, can you tell me why you faked your own death? Was it only to get out of the business while you were still the King? ... couldn't you just retire -- kind of fade out, instead of going through the trauma of dying?"

"Retire!" John shoots back. "You don't just retire from being the King. I was the King and I believed that. I had so much vanity, such a strong ego about it that no one was going to be able to get my head out of the clouds. It had been discussed before, but there was no possibility of it ever happening. If I had tried retirement I would still have remained in the public's eye. I'd never have been free, never left alone by the media people or the success hunters.

"I'd have been the King, at least to myself, all the time. There would also have been the challenge of the younger competition and I'd have had to face that challenge, in the end becoming nobody -- a 'has been'. That would never have been for me anymore than I could have been successful at retirement; it was all or nothing. So everything would have continued just the way it was. This left me only one way out and I thank God it worked.

"It's very difficult to explain to people how it feels to wear gold and diamonds on your fingers and chains of useless pride around your neck out of vanity. If I didn't carry a mirror in my pocket all the time, then someone must have carried it for me. I'm sure there are some people who would be able to identify with what I'm telling you. It needs to be experienced to be really understood."

"Do you blame anyone for causing you to take drugs, or lose touch with the truth about what was happening to you?"

"I did for some time before the escape plan was put into effect and during the debriefing sessions. As far as I was concerned, it certainly wasn't me; after all, look at the demands they put on me."

"Who is they? You mean the fans?"

"Yes, but mostly the producers, managers, writers, directors and everyone else connected with the shows. "Act this way"... "Sing this way"... "Do this interview"... "Appear here and appear there".... Everywhere I went I needed bodyguards. I was constantly in need of protection -- to get in to play a concert and again to get out. I was constantly surrounded by people. It became so bad that when I was left alone I couldn't take it because I wasn't the center of anyone's attention -- I craved an audience -- I was a star! If I was a rock and roll giant, there must be people around me to recognize it -- or so

I came to believe. It turned me into some sort of an addict -- I was addicted to being center stage! I had become so accustomed to having people around me all the time that if I wasn't performing before an audience, and it didn't matter if there were ten or ten thousand in the audience, just so long as I had the spotlight, I was bored!

"I'm sure you've heard about me shooting out TV sets at Graceland. Well, that's true. For me it wasn't a display of emotional instability, it was an attention getter!"

"Wait, John, let me get this straight. Are you saying you craved the stimulus of center stage *all the time?* Wasn't this very attention what caused you to leave the business?"

"Yes sir, that's correct! How can I make you understand ... although I loved to perform and I loved my audience, there was a part of me hated it. At least that's the way it was the last few years ... before I got out.

"But in answer to your question about blame, nobody was really responsible for what was happening to me, not the fans nor anyone else. It was me. I was the one who had lost the ability to control my life. After all, there are lots of entertainers out there who have gone through similar experiences and came out just fine.

"I've thought about it a lot. Why wasn't I able to take it all in my stride? The only answer I can come up with is that I didn't really want it in the first place."

"Would you do it again if given the chance?"

"I wouldn't want to be offered that choice."

"John, I understand during those last years prior to 1977, that you had a great deal of trouble remembering the words to your songs and that just getting on stage presented a serious problem. Can you tell me about that?"

"Yes, that was just one more of the problems I was facing in my life at that time. It's true about forgetting words in my songs. It's also true that just getting me out of a hotel bed before a performance was a serious problem. You see, I was taking pills to sleep, to wake up, to stay awake ... you name it, I was taking it. My energy level was low; I was overweight and I was very depressed; probably because of all the medications I was taking.

"The situation was almost to the point of canceling some of my shows at the last minute. You know, Bill, a lot of people are under the impression that I wasn't aware of the condition I was in, but they're wrong. It's true that in some circumstances I lost all awareness, but for the most part, I knew what was happening to me."

"Were you, or did you feel suicidal during that period?"

John hesitated, walked over to the fireplace and added another log before answering Bill's question. "I'm not sure that even those people closest to me knew how deep the depression had grown. I thought of it many times. Bill, have you ever been depressed, I mean really depressed? Do you have any idea what it's like? Let me try to describe just a few moments of what I felt.

"It was mid-winter and I was at Graceland. Late one night I walked outside and looked up at the stars. The night sky was black and the stars were as bright as twinkling diamonds on a bed of black velvet. A cold swirling breeze surrounded me. I thought for a moment how beautiful the sky was that night when all of a sudden I realized how cold and lonely the night sky appeared ... all those stars were suddenly without life. The breeze wrapped around me like an icy black hand holding me tight and whispering to me, *You have gold and silver, diamonds and pleasures, but I have you now.* There I stood, totally alone. I was to feel those icy black fingers and that black hand of depression cover me for many years.

"I remember thinking that night, 'I can shake this, I'll just go back into the house where it's warm ... people are there who will protect me.'

"But it wasn't to be; the house ... my friends ... no one offered any consolation -- there was no relief. Anxiety increased with the depression and loneliness. It seemed as if there was just no way out of it."

Chapter 9

John's voice is filled with emotion as he continues his saga. "You know that voice that whispered to me? Well, it wasn't a supernatural phenomenon kind of thing -- it was my own voice. You see, I was aware all the time of my own shame, even with the drugs and the confusion that I felt. I *knew* I had taken advantage of a lot of people."

"Can you elaborate on that for me, John. What do you mean by taking advantage of people?"

"It was the business -- the stardom. I was the king and could do no wrong. Anything I wanted, someone was always there to okay it. I could have any girl and all the sex I could take. I could, and did, get all the drugs my body had developed a craving for.... Money? -- if I couldn't buy it, I didn't need it -- or so my mind was programmed to think.

"You remember when I told you that I used to forget the words to my music? Well, as far as I was concerned I was so great that if they had propped me up and rolled me onto the stage, the audience would have been satisfied. Yes, I took advantage and I hurt a lot of folks, but most of all I hurt myself. My fall was imminent, self-destruction was inevitable."

John stopped, lowered his head as if in shame, then looked back up to

Bill. "You know, Bill, all those fans that came to see me perform didn't realize how much I envied them. I remember signing autographs for them. They seemed to glow with a sort of excitement when they were around me. Oh, how I was tempted to say to them, 'It's you who have it all, not I!', but I never could get myself to say it out loud; instead I let it eat at my insides while I continued to lean on drugs to keep me from screaming, 'It's enough, I want no more of it!"

"John, I've noticed that you live a modest sort of life, I mean, your home here and your car.... Do you still receive royalties from the Graceland Museum or your records?"

"No. Money is not a problem; I have plenty of that. I take a modest allowance each month and seldom need more than that. When I left the business, I left everything behind. I don't need or want any of the rewards that may still be building up from my success."

"You've talked about the drugs and the depression. What about your friends? Couldn't they have been helpful in your times of need?"

"Yes ... I could have listened to them, but I didn't *hear* them. You see I never ... or seldom at best, was able to recognize their concern for me, not even their friendship.

"It wasn't always that way, just gradually developed during the later years -- due to my drugged mental state, I suppose. Since most of the people surrounding me were also on the payroll, how could they be my real friends?

I was starting to lose touch with reality by then and with it went the intimacy of true friendship. I mistrusted everyone that was close to me. Granted, it was part of my own confused perception of things, but to me it was very real -- how can you have true friends when you are paying them to be there? How can you, or anyone, possibly understand that?

"So for me, there was no one I could talk to ... no one who could understand how I felt. Only later, much later, after I went into counseling, was I be able to see how wrong I'd been. There really were a lot of folks that cared a great deal about me -- but it was too late; the damage was beyond repair -- there was no turning back the clock. I wasn't able to identify with them during those bad times."

"It appears, John, that guilt became a large part of your life. I mean, you didn't, or weren't able to deal with the mistakes and wrong-doings, is that correct?"

"Yes sir. I was brought up with a good, sound moral foundation. God was a part of my life and instrumental in all my reactions to fame, especially during that period of my life. Finally, my conscience refused to compromise or accept that way of life. You might say, my soul rebelled."

Bill's glance shifts to the Bible on the end table next to his chair. He reaches over and picks it up. It falls open to a page where John has inserted a marker and underlined a passage,"What profit a man who hath gained the whole world, but has lost his soul."

Bill looks back up to John, "Are you a religious man?"

"Yes sir, I always have been. That is, until I misplaced it for awhile, you know, like put it in a drawer and lock it up. I never found the key again 'til I broke loose from my music and all the fame and heartache that came with it."

"Do you attend church now?"

"Oh yes, every Sunday my good friend and I attend."

"And your good friend is who?"

"Mona. We are close, been good friends for quite a few years now. She's a special lady."

"I'd like to meet her."

"Oh, you will -- in fact, how about tomorrow?"

"Good ... great! I'd like that very much. John, I want to ask you about Priscilla, if that's all right with you?"

John's reply is immediate. "No! I'll discuss my own personal sensitivities, but not those involving other people in my previous life. They deserve my discretion. I won't spotlight them, not even for you."

"I understand, but I'd still like to ask about your mother -- is that okay?"

"You can ask; I may not answer."

Bill proceeds. "It's my understanding that when your mother died, it impacted your life very strongly, even your career was never the same after that. Is that true?" John nods his head. "How did it change things for you?"

John hesitates before answering this probing question. "My mother was my best friend. She was everything that represented honesty, truth, and innocence in my life. She was always proud of me. Her gentleness and unblemished character were never touched by my success. I would've given her the moon had she not died. Mom was always there for me. She never asked for anything and her concern was for my happiness and well-being. She never interfered with anything I did, but was there whenever I needed her. I could tell when she disapproved of a decision; like ... if I hired someone she didn't like or trust for some reason, or if I was about to get involved in something over my head, Mom was there. Though she said little at the time, when we were alone she'd express her feelings [not giving me advice, mind you] on the subject, but that was sufficient for me to reconsider my decision.

"She was never loud or bluntly critical; she just gently told me how she felt about a matter, and that was enough to turn on a light in my brain. I always respected her advice and often acted on it.... I came to depend on her to keep me on track ... and, yes, I still miss her very much." John has expressed his thoughts showing the emotion such memories awaken.

"Do you think your mom would approve of your present way of life?"

"That's a little difficult to answer because my career probably would not have gone quite the way it did. I think success would still have come, but my personal life would not have ended the way it did.

"I'm sure she'd never have let me become hooked on drugs ... probably I'd still be on stage ... and at the top. In death, I'm certain she would be happy with the way it all evolved. Mom would be happy that I was given a second chance; she would approve of my life as it is today, too."

"You loved her very much...."

"I still do," John says, softly repeating as if to himself, "I still do."

"What about your father? Wasn't he just as prominent in your life, providing for your needs along with your mother?"

"My father was a different type of person. He was there for me, but it wasn't the same. I wish I could do better than that for an answer, but for now, let's leave it there. My father is still very special to me. Maybe we can take this up at a later time."

"That's okay. Any regrets, I mean about leaving the busines and all?"

"No, how could I regret a life filled with anxiety, frustration, substance abuse and self-deceit? Oh, I sometimes think of the concerts and the magic they generated, but it's just a fleeting thought. I'm happy now, that's what counts. I wouldn't change my life today for anything."

"Why do you feel so strongly about exposure? Are you sure that you're willing to face a future without all the glamour surrounding your past? Do you realize you may even be forfeiting the life you lead here for headlines and pressure from the press and your fans?"

"I have considered all that -- wouldn't have called you if I didn't realize and accept the possible consequences."

"Do you have any idea how you would handle such a situation?"

"I wish I knew -- I'm hoping it won't come to that. Just in the last few nights I've been experiencing nightmares and flashbacks. I had some trouble with those for about a year after I started my new life, but they had subsided. Now they've come back, mostly distorted and full of camera flashes, colored lights, loud music and people -- all kinds of people. Their voices converge, some screaming, some firing questions at me, and all at the same time. Everybody wants something and I don't have enough to go around. They drain me until there's nothing left and I wake up soaked in sweat, and yes, scared, afraid of what's about to come.

"I don't want to become vulnerable as a result of the story you are about to set loose, yet I know it's coming -- I expect it. From here on I will have to rely on my own strength to deal with it."

"Do you think you can you do that? Are you emotionally ready for the story to explode?"

John walks over to the sliding glass doors, calls Sunny over, and lets him out to take care of business, then turns and answers Bill's questions.

"I don't have any choice as I see it? I have to do this!" he says with determination in his voice. He pauses for a long moment, then continues, "I'm depending on something bigger than myself this time -- on God to carry me through -- otherwise I'm not sure I could survive it."

Bill stands up, walks over to the piano, pulls the seat out and sits down facing John. He looks into his face and feels certain he is no longer talking with

Elvis Presley, but to a product called John. Distinctly, there are only two men in the room, one is Bill Davis, the reporter and the other is John! Clearly, the shadow of Elvis Presley is no longer present, it is dead and buried. He was a talented man who became a victim of his own success and everything that went with it, and now his time is past.

Bill was full of excitement before arriving for this meeting and the interview. He felt almost like a teenager being introduced to his idol for the very first time. He had mused, "What will I say to him?" "What will I ask him?" "How will I behave toward this man?" "Wow, Elvis Presley!"

Now, facing the man, it wasn't like that at all. Two people, first Elvis and now this person John, separated only by history and time. No matter what happens now, that will not change, nor should it. Elvis will not be brought back and John must survive; he, Bill Davis, was chosen to separate them, assuring life to only one of them -- John.

Still standing by the glass doors, waiting for his dog to come back in, John, looking out, breaks the silence. "I think the rain is coming in again. It's been this way for about a week now -- on again, off again, but it doesn't seem to want to end."

Suddenly, there is a loud crack of thunder over the house followed by the lights going off, then a flash of white lightening which silhouettes John. For a split second, Bill sees what appears to be an apparition of something that once was. Bill is taken by surprise at this ghostly sight. What he saw is impossible;

he knows better than to believe in ghosts -- it must have been a memory, he justifies to himself, not a ghost from the past.

What would happen when the story was released? Would anyone be so foolish as to attempt to add substance to a memory? Would they try to pour life into a ghost? Or would they dress him in a sparkling white jump suit, set up a stage, and shine the bright spotlight of yesterday on him, shouting, *Sing, Elvis, sing!... take us back to yesterday!... you can do it, we know you can!*

Bill's thoughts are interrupted by the scratching of John's dog at the door. John lets him in. "Getting a little wet out there, huh, Sun?"

The lights flicker and come back on. Bill asks John, "How do you feel about calling it a night? It's getting pretty late."

"Sure."

"I'm looking forward to meeting your friend tomorrow -- Mona, isn't it?"

"Mona...?" repeats John, as if coming out of a daze.

"Yes, I'd like very much to talk with her if you don't mind. Maybe I can get another perspective on your lifestyle."

"I'll call her in the morning. Your bedroom has everything you need and you know where the bathroom is. Help yourself to anything in the house while you're here."

"Thanks, John. You are an excellent host. See you in the morning. Goodnight."

John starts toward his bedroom but is interrupted by Bill's voice.

"John ... don't worry about the story ... we'll do it right.... Okay?"

John smiles, "Okay -- and thanks!"

As Bill prepares to retire, he thinks how a couple of phone calls and one day with John has focused all his efforts and experience as a reporter on John's incredible life story.

He has had to read between the lines of their conversation and scrutinize John's facial and body expressions very carefully in a few brief moments before making what could turn out to be a life-or-death decision.

Is he biting off too large a chunk this time? He weighs this thought for a moment ... then smiles as he reaches his conclusion ... he has just been handed his favorite dessert.

"Yes, Bill, you have just undertaken the biggest challenge of your life."

Chapter 10

Morning breaks for the two men. Rain is gently tapping on the windows. John is already in the kitchen preparing coffee and getting Sunny's food out. Bill wanders into the kitchen, extends a cheerful good morning and informs John that he's heading for the shower.

"Coffee will be ready whenever you are," says John.

"Thanks. I'll make this one short," replies Bill.

John starts to pick up the phone to call Mona when it rings. John answers and a voice says, "Hello ... how are you?"

"I'm fine and was just about to call you, but you beat me," he answers.

"Ah, that's a switch for a change. How did your first meeting go?"

"Well, I like the man, Mona. He listens without pressuring me."

"Good! -- sounds like you picked the right person."

"Yes, I think so. I slept well last night and that's something I haven't done in a couple of nights. He'd like to meet you. Can you come over here, or would you prefer that we come out to your place?"

"Have you had breakfast yet?"

"No, why?"

"Well, I could come over and cook it for you, or maybe we could go out for breakfast ... what do you think?"

"Why don't you come on over. We'll eat here and maybe we can go out for lunch later?"

"Great! that makes sense. Anything I can pick up for you on my way?"

"Hmn ... yes, you can. I'm out of orange juice."

"Nothing else?"

"Nope. We're pretty well stocked."

"I'll be there in about half an hour. I'm glad everything went well, John. Maybe now things will turn around for you. I prayed very hard for that last night."

"Thanks, so did I. See you soon, Mona. Bye."

Bill has finished showering and is dressed when he returns to the kitchen.

"Bill, how do you like your coffee? Cream, sugar, black?"

"Black will be fine. Thanks." Bill says as he sits down at the kitchen table.

"Mona is on her way over to cook breakfast for us -- unless you'd rather eat out?"

"No, thank you, home cooking sounds great. I spend so much time eating out that sometimes I skip meals rather than go into another restaurant. A meal prepared at home will be a real treat."

"You know, John, I envy your lifestyle here. You have a home and everything you need in it. You have beautiful surroundings and apparently a nice lady who even cooks for you."

John smiles, "Yes, I do. Are you married?"

"Yes, I'm married, but we don't see as much of each other as we'd like to. I spend as many as twelve hours a day at the network preparing news stories; my wife works, but it's only for something to do. I think she'd go crazy if she didn't work. Sometimes I wonder if we will ever get to spend some good quality time together."

"I'm sorry to hear that. Circumstances don't always provide everything we would like to have, do they?"

"No, I guess not. Someday I hope things will change for us. It just seems I'm so locked in to my work and everything."

John looks closely at Bill. "Just remember, you also possess the key, just as I finally realized I did. Do you understand?"

Bill smiles. "Yeah, I guess I do. You are a wise man, John. No matter what happens, I'll always consider it a privilege to have met you."

Embarrassed by the compliment, John replies, "We're all wise, Bill, only sometimes it takes a little longer to tune in to it. You're not so very different from me. We all seek our own success and there's always a price tag at the end. It's a matter of how long we can hang in before the decision is finally reached to turn our lives in another direction; generally, that time comes out of desperation -- when we realize the old way just isn't working. The timing, however, is not the same for everyone. For me it was when all the other doors had closed and only this one remained ... and I walked through it.

"What if your marriage goes bad as a result of your pursuit of success? By then it may be too late to re-evaluate the true price you have paid? So, although circumstances may differ, the story remains the same. In my case, success was quite costly, almost to the point of taking my own life, and it just wasn't worth it anymore!"

There was a knock on the door, breaking this moment of soul-searching for Bill.

"Come on in. We're in the kitchen."

"Hello, here's the juice."

"Thanks, hon." He turns and says, "Bill, this is Mona ... and Mona, this is Bill Davis."

"I've been looking forward to this meeting, Mona. How are you?"

"Very well, thank you, Bill. So have I." Jokingly she adds, "Has John been talking about me again?"

"Unfortunately, no. That's why I wanted to meet you."

"Let me get out of this coat and I'll start breakfast. Why don't the two of you take your coffee into the living room. That will give me some space."

"Okay, you're the boss," John replies, "the kitchen is now officially all yours. Your hair is wet, want a towel?"

"No, it won't help. I'll try to fix it again later."

John and Bill take their coffee and retreat, as ordered, to the living room.

"Well, Bill, I'm sorry about the weather. I'd wanted to show you around the lake, maybe do a little fishing. By the way, do you like to fish?"

"I haven't fished in at least five years, but I used to love it -- still do, but time is a demanding employer and leaves very little of it for catching fish."

"Listen, Bill, no matter what else happens, anytime you would like to come back, you'd be welcome. Maybe we could arrange for a hunting trip or do some fishing -- whatever you'd like -- maybe include your wife, I'm sure Mona would like that too."

"I'll take you up on that offer and thanks again."

Mona's head pops around the kitchen divider, "Hon, you don't have any eggs either, the carton is there but it's empty -- you should have looked before saying no when I asked you."

"Sheepishly, John says, "I'm sorry, I thought the box was full."

"It will only take me a few minutes to pick up a carton."

"Do you want me to go?"

Mona smiles teasingly, "Please?"

"John, does that mean I get to be alone with this beautiful lady?"

John laughs as he answers, "Yes, I guess it does, but remember, Sunny is very protective of my friends!"

"Oh? then I'll have to be very careful, won't I?"

"I'll be back in a jiffy."

"Take your time," Bill remarks as he walks back to the kitchen.

"Mona, how do you feel about all this? I mean, the story going public and all?"

"It doesn't seem to be a question of choice, I wish it were. Although," she hesitates, "I'm not as convinced as John is that the Johnsons will talk."

"Johnson -- is that the name of the person he is worried about?"

"Yes, hasn't he told you about them?"

"No. He only touched on the word 'neighbor', but hasn't gone into any detail about them. What's it all about?"

"Two summers ago, a couple purchased a cabin about a half mile north of here. They come down from Toronto to spend part of the summer months here. He is apparently a retired fire chief from a city in the States. They seem to be pleasant enough. While they're here they sometimes rent a boat from me. They like to spend a few hours on the lake. John has told me that on several occasions they appear to behave somewhat strangely when they see him."

"How does it show?" Bill asks.

"Well, I know that on one occasion, when I was with John doing some grocery shopping, we acknowledged each other in the store and went about our business. We were picking up something from a shelf on the opposite side of the isle from where they were and they couldn't see us, but we heard her asking him if they should tell someone. We heard him say, "Tell who?"

We weren't able to hear more of the conversation, but John swears that every time he runs into them, they greet him and move off, and seem to be whispering to each other, even staring right at him as they talk.

Since I have known John, he has never been overly concerned about things like that. He handles his suspicions very well, but this time it's different. I'm sure there are folks here, who've known him for some time, who may be suspicious of his resemblance to someone they once knew. However, if they do suspect something, they certainly are not talking, thank goodness!"

So you are not totally convinced that the Johnsons would expose him?"

"I really don't know. I wish I did."

"Well, at least I know a little more about it now and that helps. Tell me, Mona, how do *you* feel about John? I mean, the man he was ... and who he is today."

"As to who he was, that's history; not much I can tell you about Elvis Presley ... it's all in the books. As for the person he is today, well ... first of all I love him very much. He's a compassionate, kind, sensitive person. I think he is still insecure about himself, but that is to be expected. He has always known that some day it might come down to this and he's always handled it very well. He never let it eat at him until recently."

With a deep sigh, Mona continues, "But then, maybe what's about to happen and the fact that you're doing the story is all for the best."

"Do you really believe that?"

Mona doesn't answer the question.

"Why aren't you two married?"

"Oh, I think maybe he's waiting for what he feels is the right time. I don't think John wants me to be exposed to what might happen if he was found out some day. I'd like to see him through this as his wife. Maybe if your story is accepted ... well ... then we can finally get married."

"He's a very lucky man to have you by his side through all this."

Smiling, Mona says, "Thank you. He's already been through more than most people in a lifetime. He scrambled in the mud then rode on a cloud and had everything in between. After all that, he's entitled to live the rest of his life as he chooses."

Mona, suddenly sounding angry, says, "God! I wish there were no people in the world like the Johnsons! Why *are* there such people -- why can't they leave well enough alone -- why do they have to stir up trouble to get their kicks!

Quietly, Mona apologizes to Bill, "I'm sorry, I didn't mean to sound off like that."

"You've nothing to be sorry for. I understand and I feel for both of you. I've come to like John very much. He's a special kind of man."

"Yes, he is, isn't he?" Mona answers, her face suddenly lighting up.

John arrives with the eggs. "Now we can really have breakfast!"

Mona takes the eggs from John, "Why don't you two get out of my kitchen? Go! Shoo ... back to the living room -- talk or whatever so I can get this food on the table. It'll only be a few minutes."

John and Bill, pretending to cringe, return to the living room once again.

Bill, still laughing, points out, "She is very special ... and you, John, are a very lucky man to have found her."

"Yes sir, I know I am."

Sitting down again, they pick up their conversation where they left off when John went 'egg-hunting'.

"She is special! ... and you are a lucky man!"

"Yes sir, I certainly am."

They talk about generalities for awhile, until Bill says, "John, I'm going back to New York tomorrow. I don't want to, but it's necessary."

"But you just got here last night! Do you have enough material to do the story? You didn't tape or video ... or anything."

"I know, John. I didn't have to. I've given this a lot of thought. I may have gotten all of a half hour's sleep last night."

"But ..."

"Hear me out, John."

Mona, becoming aware of the conversation, anxiously enters the living room as Bill continues, "Both of you listen to me. I've come to a decision. There are several options here for you. I'll discuss them later on, but for now, the reason I'm going back tomorrow is my boss. He's a man who's been a friend of mine for many years. He's expecting to hear from me by tomorrow, but instead of calling him, I'd like to face him. You see, he has taken a negative view of this interview. First of all, he doesn't think your phone call was legitimate. Secondly, as it were, he was coming after you without any consideration. I'm sure you understand what I'm talking about."

John drops his head in his hands.

"What good, then, was all of this?" Mona asks.

"I understand your anxiety, please settle down for a moment. I can handle my boss. Don't be concerned about that. Let me assure you that everything will be all right."

"How?" John wants to know.

"Look, why don't we have breakfast and spend the day the way you normally would, as if I weren't here. You trusted me enough to call me to do your story, don't stop now."

Bill smiles at both of them, "Now, you go finish your cooking. I'll tell both of you later about how I want to handle this, okay?"

"It appears we have no other choice ... okay."

"Good! Now how about it? What do you have planned for us after we've eaten?" Bill asks.

"Well, I'm not exactly sure. I haven't entertained guests in my home for a long time. I'm not sure I remember how, and besides, it's raining. Any ideas, Mona?" John raises his voice so Mona can hear him.

"Come and get it!" then, as they sit town, Mona continues, "Let's take a drive around to the Islands. It'll be fun ... rain and all! "We'll take my Blazer, have a late lunch on the road, and spend the evening here. What do you think?"

"How do you feel about that, Bill?"

"Why not ... I think its a great idea. Come on, you guys, I'm hungry, let's eat."

Small talk accompanies the meal. Mona clears the table while John explains the trip they are taking. "It's not a real long drive and I think you will enjoy the sights. There are a few beautiful spots where you can see hundreds of islands sitting out in the lake. Mona and I often take the boat over and explore some of them. A few even have cabins built on them."

Finished eating and straightening up the kitchen, Mona turns to the two of them, saying, "I'm all set, hon. You boys ready?"

"Ready," Bill answers, "let's get going."

"Let's take Sunny, he can sit in the back with me. Bill, you sit up front with John."

Chapter 11

As they drive through the countryside, John and Mona fill Bill in on some of the anecdotes of their previous trips.

"You see that farm over there? Mona has me drive her out here whenever the strawberries are in season. She picks a boxful and eats them before we ever get home."

Bill laughs, "Must be delicious when they're fresh-picked."

"You bet. Next time you're here, we'll drive out just to pick them. You'll be just as tempted as I am to sink your teeth into them."

"My mouth is already watering for a taste."

Bill abruptly changes the subject, "Mona, tell me, is John a funny guy? I got the impression that he had a great sense of humor when he interrupted our long distance conversation, asking me to hold the line while he went to feed Sunny."

John glances back at Mona with a smile, "Am I a funny person?"

Mona thinks for a moment, then says, "Yes, I believe he is at times. There are even moments when he still pokes fun at his old self -- in fact, he can still swivel a mean pelvis." She ends up with a laugh as she remembers one or two such demonstrations.

Bill's questions are not asked in an interview format. They are more general in tone, requiring no specific response. Curiosity rather than anything else is his motive as he pursues his questioning.

"What about humility, Mona?"

"Plenty of that -- he has an awareness of it. Still, he has showmanship qualities as well which, I believe, he must have had to begin with -- both characteristics are part of his personality and what made him such a success with the fans."

Bill glances over at John who returns his glance with a somewhat sheepish shrug and upraised eyebrows.

Not hearing any objection from John, she continues, "I think that even as a 'your man' John was humble, even shy, but he also had a natural ability to perform so when the door to fame opened, his innate showmanship qualities made him an instant hit and ... he simply clicked!"

"John, weren't your sideburns and hair a little out of place when you were in school? I think you told me that you got into trouble on more than one occasion because of them."

"Yeah, I guess so, but I preferred to think of myself in my early years as different rather than a showoff."

As the tour goes on and John and Mona continue to point out the sights, Bill is struck by their mutual ties and the simplicity of their lives. For a moment he, too, is caught up in their lives and will dwell with nostalgia on this visit with the passage of time.

They have spent time standing out in the rain to see the countryside, eating together, sharing anxiety, memories and laughter, all rolled into one short span of time. Bill has shaken the hand of a legend and spoken with the end product of what was once the King. It could not have turned out any better for him.

Elvis Presley had been given a 'second chance'." How many of us would get that and then pass it up? Elvis might have passed it by without recognizing the opportunity it presented, but John had taken over and it is now John who is trying to make the most of his new life.

It is about seven o'clock when they return to John's house. As they go inside, Mona asks John if he would like her to leave so they can talk.

"No," Bill interrupts, "please stay. What I have to say concerns both of you now."

John arm encircles Mona's waist as they wait for Bill to continue.

"Okay," says Mona, "I'd like it that way. John, why don't you start a fire and I'll make some coffee. Would anyone like a sandwich?"

Both men speak up at once, "Maybe later, but coffee sure sounds good."

Bill sits down and Sunny stretches out on the floor in front of him. They have become good friends by now. He reaches down and pets the large Husky.

"I've enjoyed this day more than words can describe. It's been a long time since I've felt so relaxed and comfortable."

Mona comments, "It's nice to have you here, Bill and I want to thank you for including me in the circle."

As John prepares the fire, Bill chuckles, "You know, John, you never did let me meet Elvis."

John hesitates as he kneels to light the fire, turns his head toward Bill and says, "If you were able to stay a little longer, maybe you would catch a glimpse of him." Smiling, John continues, "I'm afraid that's about all that's left of him."

"I understand, John," Bill says, not without emotion, and with a great deal of warmth in his voice.

Mona brings the coffee in and sits down.

"John, will you sing for me?" asks Bill.

John is taken by surprise at this request. He looks over at Mona who nods her head in agreement.

Slowly, John walks over to the old piano, sits down, looks at the keys for a few seconds, then starts to play the notes to one of his favorite songs, *Amazing Grace.*

Bill settles into his chair as John sings the words. There is no doubt today of this man's priorities.

As he finishes singing, Bill softly remarks, "I've never heard the song sung so beautifully and with such presence." Bill is not known to be a particularly religious person, but as he hears John sing he is briefly put in touch with his own spirituality.

John ends the song and Bill, as if awakened from a trance, exclaims, "You may have touched the ears of angels with that, John!"

John answers, "I've been trying to for a long time."

Mona asks, "Will you sing another?"

"Maybe -- a little later. I'm a little anxious to continue our earlier conversation. Bill, how do you intend to handle this story?"

"Okay, I want you both to listen carefully. When I get back to New York, I'm going to write the story. I'm going to write about everything I've seen and heard here. I'm also going to write about my feelings of this experience.

"John ... Mona.... This is one of the easiest and yet the most difficult assignments I've ever undertaken. It's also been one of the best experiences of my life.

Bill takes a deep breath and begins, "John, I don't think this story should be told at all -- at least not right now."

John starts to interrupt ... but is stopped by Bill.

"Let me finish, John. Mona has told me about the Johnsons -- a concern of major importance to you. Your fears may be justified, however, if I am correct, they have spent two summers here without an apparent leak. If something should come out, we'll be ready for it. Let's not, however, do it now. You have lived here a number of years without incident; we don't need to jump the gun now. It's not as impossible as you may think to be left alone to live the life you have chosen. You've done it this long, why not continue? The two of you may want to approach the Johnsons next summer and subtly feel them out, or even be straight with them. That is your decision. No matter what happens, you have nothing to lose.

"John, I assure you that I will be prepared to air the story at the first sign of trouble. I'll do everything in my power to help you keep it from being told. However, if that time should come, all you have to do is say the word."

John looks at Mona, "What do you think?"

"What's to think about? As Bill just told us, what do you have to lose? Maybe your story will never have to be told at all. We both know that our prayers have been answered before, including," she smiles at Bill, "bringing you to us."

John stands up and walks over to Bill. He puts his hand out to shake Bill's, but spontaneously wraps both arms around Bill in a great big bear hug. "Okay, we'll do it your way and thanks ... but what about your boss?"

"My returning early will add some credibility to what I'm going to tell him. You see, part of his objection to my coming out here was simply that I was on a wild goose chase. That's exactly what I'm going to tell him. I'll get an 'I told you so' and it will be forgotten.

After a moment of silence in the room, Mona says, "Anybody for a ham sandwich?" Her voice is pure music with the relief of this decision.

John and Bill look at each other, then at Mona, "What are we waiting for,

I'm famished," John says, clinching the discussion.

"Coming right up."

"So, it's over. When did you decide you were not going to print the story?"

"That's a little hard to pinpoint, but I think it started after I spoke to my boss about coming here. His attitude about the possibility of you still being alive, and how the story would be handled if it were true, surprised me as well as angering me. Then, when I met you the first time, the notion was reinforced, although I didn't know until last night how I would suppress the story. Finally, when Mona told me about the Johnsons, it all came together and that was when I *really* decided the story should not be told at all.

Mona enters the room with a plate of sandwiches. Placing the tray on the table, she asks Bill why he chose not to video tape the interview.

"It wasn't exactly clear to me at the time, but when I realized that we might not have to air the story at all, it became evident that if and when things changed and John's story might have to be told, I didn't want any photographic evidence to go with it. Plastering your face on the television networks around the world would bring instant recognition, something that must, in my opinion, be totally avoided."

They munched on their sandwiches, each absorbed by their own thoughts, but before long the conversation picked up again, changing to small talk. A tremendous weight has just been lifted, not just from John's shoulders, but from Mona's and Bill's as well.

Mona and John will be able to move on with their lives; Bill is relieved, at least for the present, of doing a story he really didn't want to do. Exposing this man and his life to the world with the definite possibility of dire consequences, was not Bill's idea of good reporting. He had developed a great respect for John and everything he'd been through before arriving at this point in his life. Then there was Mona -- they were so obviously in love, but until now happiness had seemed totally hopeless.

His personal liking for John began with their first meeting when John found Bill sitting on his doorstep. It had deepened with each conversation, and eventually, it had included his friend, Mona.

As the three sit talking, John ponders the last few days that started with a decision and a long distance phone call in the rain. He remembers his fear, his deep depression. He felt again, after many years of a happy life, the cold, black fingers of depression about to strangle him. He recalls thinking, *What would Bill be like? Would he be able, or even try, to understand when John tells him the story?* Those unknowns weighed heavily on John before Bill arrived. Now it was over. They had found a workable solution to the problem; a solution John would be able to live with. Bill had the story; the Johnsons may not talk; secrecy may very well prevail....

They spent the next three hours talking as friends. Mona finally left about eleven o'clock to finish up some last minute paperwork on her business. She and Bill exchanged an affectionate hug intertwined with Mona warmly thanking him for salvaging their lives with the answer to a monstrous puzzle. Mona hugged and kissed John, saying happily, "Now we can see each other for the rest of our lives."

"I'll be leaving early in the morning, John. You have my sincere envy for the life you have carved out for yourself. I've never met a more interesting man. I hope life will always be good to you and Mona -- you have certainly earned it!"

John nods his head and smiles his appreciation for Bill's kind words. "See you in the morning, sleep well."

"You too."

John wakes up at 5:45 a.m. and decides to wake Bill up too. As he passes the dining room table, he eyes catch the note.

"John, no more good-byes. I'll be in touch. Thanks for the phone call. P.S. You'd better marry that girl, she may well be part of your second chance. Bill"

The sun will shine and the day will be crisp and bright. It's a new day and a new beginning for John. Elvis may be dead, but John is full of life and he intends to live every minute of it!